STRETCHING FENCE

STRETCHING FENCE

by Sonya Dorman

OHIO UNIVERSITY PRESS: ATHENS, OHIO

Some of the poems in this collection have appeared in the following publications: THE LITTLE MAGAZINE, Bird Frame; PERSPECTIVE, New Roof on My Neighbor's House; UT REVIEW, Notes From Bonne Bay, Newfoundland; SATURDAY REVIEW, No, Madam, I Won't Take Anything From the Garden; THE HARTFORD COURANT, A Poem For Michiko; SOUTH FLORIDA REVIEW, City Storm; POETRY NORTHWEST, Family Poem, Stretching Fence on Our Anniversary, Some Observations, The Mysterious Dr. Morning, Amateur: A Story, Carrying the Morning: A New England Biography; THE PAINTED BRIDE QUARTERLY, Fare Wells; OPEN PLACES, Love in the North, Province of Lonely Hunters: A New England Biography, Pigs and All; NEW DIRECTIONS 25, The Eighth Sea Journal, The Women of Town Street; ARTS IN SOCIETY, Wall Paintings: A Short History of Civilization; POETRY NOW, Early To Fish

I would like to express my gratitude to The MacDowell Colony where many of these poems were written.

Library of Congress Catalog Number: 75-14550
ISBN 0-8214-0188-2 Cloth 0-8214-0209-9 Paper
Manufactured in the United States of America

Designed by Harold M. Stevens

FOR JERRY

CONTENTS

ONE

TWO

THREE

ONE

FAMILY POEM

Oh you, your rank determination,
that of the beaver to dam his pond,
of the heron to stand all day for one fish,
of the horse radish to wait out seven winters
and multiply underground;
oh you, in ridged boots,
a strong stamp on entering
is your signature.

Oh myself, training words on trellises
with bloody fingers
so you won't know which of us blooms,
all day alive at the top
of the house where ceilings fall;
oh myself, cutting away streamside brush,
forcing the waters to the sea,
brooking no dam that holds them back
and burning bridges which cross them.

And she comes in, oh you her father
and I her mother, she, blazing with road dust,
displaying in the hot noon
every thorn, gall, and fruit
we ever wished on her;
that seedling who, as we mind
the house and the land,
thrives well enough to burst from us.

Oh you and I on a May morning
beating the ground we live on
in a rage to bring forth the beans,
the sweet peas of our marriage;
what shall we do in the grape arbor
gone to leaf, when the need
for grapes is over?

3

STRETCHING FENCE ON OUR ANNIVERSARY

Six a.m., grass white as platinum
with cold dew;
an acre away woodpeckers drill
for breakfast.
Fence posts you drove yesterday
lift like weir stakes
in the wet air.

The roll of wire we push
leaves a wide plush track on the slope.
Stumbling, I let go.
One end whips back
striking my thigh with fire.
We go on rolling;
at the first post hook on,
cut baling wire, join with pliers
and turn the roll,
all snarls like a bad dream.

Sun's up. The aluminum look
of the metal darkens to blue;
hook on, cut, join with the pliers.
If I let go at the wrong time
the wire will snap a strip from my hide.
You lean down the slope,
I lean back, keeping our boundary taut.
Here we hang in morning silence,
hooked on, joined, rusting together.

AIR

I know everything raises a roof:
toxic breath of cellar fires,
new winds, old tempers,
firemen's axes, wreaths of hose,
waterspouts.

Air shimmers over the roofer -
invisible substance where a man
may dance, strike nails, or piano keys
to develop watertight schemes.
I hit upper or lower case,
convinced that square edges
make cleanest stories.

The man on the roof with his hammer
shores us up with shingles,
looks in, asks if I'm writing a book.
I say, "Yes."
The ivy at his heels
lifts the siding from the house.
My paper turns brown, a finch dies,
another maple takes root in the garden.

"What," he asks, "are you writing on?"
Air.

WALKING ONE MORNING

Walking one morning in the bright
I wake to a new bush
on the corner where three dogs
possess the right of way
one morning as I walk
to the corner there's a new
blue bush with big heads
all over it

someone's been planting
maybe at midnight
a secret assignation with the soil
perhaps a lunar fantasy
moonblue heads on the bush
one morning where the boys
used to short cut home

a new blue bush in sunshine
on the corner
where it used to be
dull walking
Mr Boyle comes out of his house
says how do you like
my hydrangea? and pours
a bucket of water on us

CIAO

After the redpolls go,
after I say goodbye to you
with your smell of cold melon,
your mint beard,
winter comes to the blood dark sumac.

The house cracks its knuckles.
Cousins of January celebrate frost.

Inside, at four corners,
spiders rise on sticky elevators.
A raccoon reaches in under the sink,
helps himself to the garbage.

After I say goodbye to you
I fasten on to my branch,
waiting through winter
with its held breath
and carbon paper shadows.

THE EIGHTH SEA JOURNAL

1

I wake to gold paper, white
window frames, to wonder if
clarity failed during the dream,
to worry how the clouds fared
and whether the sun has come again.

With one eye on the doorway
just like waking in childhood
(ghost with runny nose),
often in despair at rain,
I find there's yet a roof
over my head, a real floor;
not one worm in sight.

2

Triumph of separate seasons:
strawberries for breakfast,
a pair of blue herons
whose shadows swim over the lawn,
winter rinds discarded with our boots.

One by one the seeds depart,
leaving me to breathe.
Last year I threw away
our girdles, lacings, gates, porcelain;
this year I grieve for those gone.

My daughter's snotty ghost
hangs in her closet like old beads.

3

At ten, there's a message from the world:
Dear lady, may we install aluminum
storm windows against the east wind?

No. You shan't take away frames
I've lived with, no matter how
I've hoped to break them, loose shapes,
pour out lucid as moonlight
on salt water and sing hallelujah
for freedoms I've invented.

No thanks. Keep your comforts.
I'll forge my own, boiling blood
and the child's marrow in my saucepans.
The husband sword will plunge
in, temper, and cool.

4

It's too bad to squat in my garden
pulling up values by the root,
just because someone said: *you ought.*
With great care each afternoon I go back
and replant. That way, some green
continues to unfurl in my plot.
You ought to get out and see
what grows in other gardens, they say.

I've seen. Hoeing my own row
I'd like to take a whack or two elsewhere;
what's the good of weedlessness on my own
when around me Bouncing Bet, Solomon's Seal,
Viper's bugloss and Oxalis thrive?
Let them spread wildly while I bum
around on the porch with my bare feet up
and vapor condenses on the bottle in hand.
There's witchweed curling over my skull.

Northeast wind comes across the estuary.
It tunes up the television roof antenna
which sings in S-shaped waves,
sound of an enormously amplified
60-cycle hum, like pain, like shame.
As if every device in our man made world
stood up, hairs on a scared nape,
and trembled. The throb of a cut wrist.
The live wire carrying last night's
bad speech into the future where
we'll have to face it again.

Wind snores at the listener
trapped under the thin roof of her skin.
The easy answer is to rip away
the aerial and live without pictures,
but no thanks, gentlemen: I'll stay tuned.

6

At bedtime there's the ghost
of ghost stories.
The bed floats in its frame,
a long picture. Just thinking of sleep
is too good to be true,
like catching a bird with salt.
There's that moment of bedding down,
old donkeys turning and turning
in their ammoniated straw,
asleep on their feet.
Here we spend half our time
recounting the spilt beads, soured milk,
wounds, spleen, and platters of dust
the world has served us.

At bedtime, clutching the mattress purse
I burrow into my home in the treasure house.
Not a worm in sight in this dark,
I say, as if writing down a dream
or catching a ghost by the ear
or putting the lost beads back
on their string without getting
my thumb caught while the wind hums
and the green curls into brown sleep.

NO, MADAM, I WON'T TAKE ANYTHING
FROM MY GARDEN

Along the east wall built of rubble stone,
covered with ivy, the iris come up.
Green fans with a thrust rising from each
rhizome, unfolding on top: Desert Song,
Bronze Garland, Blue Lake, and Foxgrape.
From early May through June the wet tissues
crumple, withered, like hands
finished with prayer.
In a moist corner behind the lilacs
I leave Monkshood for that woman
who doesn't know sour grass is good salad.

June. On the slope behind the house
under the dogwood's whiskered green berries
drifts of daylilies open from sweet green pea-
like pods, delicious boiled and buttered.
Out come daily orange flowers with tickling
spots in their throats. I take the wilted
blossoms to simmer in my soups
while down below
thrives the Monkshood I leave for that woman
who'll lie in the sun and let weeds grow.

False Dragonhead, with serrated green edges,
rampages through bluebell and Veronica.
In August, when mildew's on the phlox and even
wild bees are weary, its raspberry-lavenders
blaze up the kitchen side where I make
a last dandelion salad before going, and I
smile at the secret
heights of Monkshood behind the lilac boughs
ready to burst into purple for that woman
who's been measuring my rose bed for a car port.

NEW ROOF ON MY NEIGHBOR'S HOUSE

Too damned early, seven in the morning,
the man climbs up the house,
his mouth puckered full of nails
like a seamstress with pins.

It's hot, this opening on a July day.
The roofer wears no shirt.
One brown arm rises,
hammerhead - a lens condensing light.

Flung from my bed by his boistrous fist
as shingles are slapped one on another
I stand at my window, see him ride
the horse of the ridgepole.
He scatters ivy and starlings.

Another lap; along the chimney a strip
of flashing. Light jumps from his hammer
to a metal edge in molten bubbles.

All morning he moves up
by handspans from the gutter,
then hangs the noon bell of the sun
on the chimney while we both celebrate,
he with a can of cold beer,
I with a mouthful of silence.

THE MYSTERIOUS DR. MORNING

That's the way you arrive,
turning plain pine into honeywood,
beset by the neighbors' little dogs
one yap at a time.

The grandfather clock strikes you
at the door,
our pains turn the other cheek
to your mercury,
your bag of blessings.

Awake in the operating theater
we need to be reminded: these
are real people behind the white masks.
Needles, knives, flash in corroboration.

You will make us cleaner than thou,
walking our dark streets
where dirty rain falls,
where joy reeks.

We called you, and waited hours.
Now, your reminiscences
at our bedside are terrible.

PLEASE SEND A PUBLICITY PHOTO

Black dots resemble my face
in the newspaper. The same warped grin.
Half the mouth clenched, half
blabbing to someone out of focus.

A false brunette paperweight
I stood for years on my father's desk.
There was no light on my face.
I wore a grave smile, a dark dress.

Pictures of my mother hanging
wash on a tenement roof,
descending to First Avenue's crypt,
miss her by a mile.

My grandmother, in sepia
wedding dress, had no pearls to wear;
she was poor, not beautiful,
carried water from a well.

Light from her cracked pitcher
spills over me.

Ancestry, the random genes,
the hearse-dark promise caught
in my eyes by a press camera,
I leave to my daughter.

Back to the sun, she stands
squinting with Instamatic veracity.
I smile because she doesn't tell me to.

A DISTANCE

Even if we were the only two stones
on a shore line
there's small chance the waves
would knock us together,
though our little cousins
the pebbles would tap tap around us
while we two smoothed rocks
might be touched once
by the webbed foot of a bird.

If we were two trees left
on a hillside, one on each slope,
it's doubtful if our branches'
shadows would meet
though in spring
our birds might mate.

Even if we sat together
at a small table in the lamplight
and shared one wine bottle,
what would we say to each other?
I might ask you to pass the salt.
You might ask me to give you bread.

EARTH ENTERING

The dog died, the bird died,
in the dark harbor of her mind
grandfather fell soundless,
and death's carbon
entered my daughter.

Her hands stretched
to clasp us
and emptiness gave back
its own shape.

She understood how
death's warp supports our loves
but refused it with a shy grin.
It took breath from her mouth
for a souvenir.

Now she walks holding on
to breath's taste
for fear we will forget it,
leaving her to carry on
her own.

LISTEN, DAUGHTERS

Boys' voices rise like wiring
through the house, carrying news
I expected to hear, the hellos
hung on each new face
like dust on the cat's whiskers.

In their swollen pants, boys knock
on the walls, pipes steaming up,
courting my daughters downstairs
and leaving stains
on the velvet couch.

I remember my early trials,
the rubbing together
on damp stone, wet ground,
hay, and smelly quilts;
listen, daughters, grab hold

of the pulse, don't let go, while I
hold the veins together in their source.

FARE WELLS

Goodbye, Andrew of dawn kisses.
Goodbye, Carmela with the flute.

In my pocket I carry
two tent pegs,
I leave the tent to you;
our heavy skillet
and squirrel pelts
left from desperate stew.

Goodbye, Aunt Razor
and Uncle Scythe,
my cuts have healed
and down at the pier
fifty sailorbirds
wave me off on my ship.

Goodbye, Father Blood,
the tide's going out,
it's half past time
to leave you
with all my books and speeches
and Mother Salt
for a lantern.

A SILENCE

Many years have piled up on the spike
of our silence, unpaid bills, leaves
of a secular bible. The distance between
our scrannel empires is overrun with mice,
soon the rats will be on us.

Notice of your death appears in daily papers,
in each issue of children's magazines,
in political journals. Notice of termination
is served on us every morning
in our private corridors and palaces.

Notice of my death will appear
in your medical journals, in the dry grass
at your doorstep, on the snake's skin,
transparant as oiled rice paper.

Notice of termination is never published.
It rises like grass from our brows.

What a long distance we never traveled;
that we imagined trains is enough for a life time,
it was too much to hope for tracks and power.

After reality has gone somewhere else
to other hungers, our tomorrow vanishes
in a feast of egg shells and gutter water.

TWO

DAYS WHEN LOVE IS ABSENT

Some days it's easier to sit,
my lips to the day's hair,
touching the bones of my face,
as if a child were with me in the room.

At times the tactile sense
is the only comfort;
feeling for light
with the hairs around my mouth
means a delicate step forward,
airy as dust rising.

Days when sunshine pours
around the red handle
of a cup, I'd rather feel
than think.
The cup fills with darkness,
a wonder,
a star shines and floats
in its emptiness.

LOVE IN THE NORTH

> North is easy.
> North is never love.
>   Richard Hugo

North is not easy
with its crisps and blunders,
but love is north,
a stove heat
keeping the brain limber.

The heart in the south
pours out like a river
loosed into waterfalls.
Here, we're used to the deep
channels where our blood goes black
under the ice's weight;
a slow, tremendous pressure
forcing it to move,
purged of algae
and making jewels of the stones.

We know the value of warmth
held in the body's small cave,
better than those who see it
glitter, fall away easy as death.

AFTER THE DOG DIED

A dark night, I went looking for comfort,
my dead dog, a feather, heart's ease,
stumbling in the woods by a dearth
of moonlight. Through fields, over walls,
all night wet to the knees with green dew.

At four a.m., when animals begin to move,
I swore I heard her bark, down by the creek.
No dog there, only the water yapping.

By first light, I thought this was how
my life would go from now on, falling
every three steps, and the dogsoul hung up
in the love briar, struggling,
unable to come back or go forth.

PIGS AND ALL

Iron hooks go through
the tendon of the hocks;
an abdominal slit releases
intestines. Pig's flesh
is lined with membrane
bright as live trout's shine
until air consumes it.
The smoking blood
runs down the drain.

It takes four seconds
for that shine to die,
twenty minutes for the chops
to fry, years for the man
to teach his boy how to hang
a pig by the hocks and slit
into its gut. The drain
swallows all, without question.

CITY STORM

It rains from here to Kansas
washing soot from corn and tomatoes.
Downstairs, the hulls of dark sedans
like whaleships are moored
in roaring gutters.
I'm bored with city rain, with rain.
As night arrives
lightning shows an apocalypse
of molten stone
and the paper white as a shroud
on my desk.

My airshaft turns to a waterfall.
Its walls ripple and squirm
like a bursting womb.
Oh Doctor Love, can you
scrape me clean?

Thunder stuns the city
to its cellars, Sunday
washes away.
I wrap my poems
in the week's trash and wait
for the blue space of dawn
when moonshine corrugates
the pond in a far park.

Monday's sun will dry
this vein, I'll forget how hard
my heart works
when the sky comes down.

WALL PAINTINGS: A SHORT HISTORY OF CIVILIZATION

In Europe I saw a rock painting
two thousand years old: the shaman
beat a drum, the woman danced.
   Here in the subway,
wall scrawls cling to dank tiles.
I hear someone following me.
     A train comes
in the tunnel on a loud wind; I'm glad
to be swallowed. Six stops. How many shamans
this tribe has, and so many deep temples.

This is the old place of fear, the cave;
toxic fumes enter my head. I'll cry out
if I stay. There's someone climbing
behind me.
     At the moment of emerging
into dark fog, an awful sorrow burns in me
because of the dream: I might have ridden
on into dawn's safety at the end of the line.
     Too late.
Footsteps double. A god or his shaman stalks;
my hide quivers while my hairs stand,
sure sign of a presence.

Each black cross street may be an altar.
And I didn't leave my mark anywhere.
How bad to die among sirens and strangers
with no name.
     Someone is running.
Her hair streams like a slate mark

on the night's surface.
      I have not been chosen.
As they pass, I see her pulling along
her bones in a skin sack, the mad god
close behind. All through the city's thickets
I look for a clean place to lie down
but even under my feet, the marks scream:
worship, and fear me.
      To propitiate
the next avatar of fate, I'll paint myself
flat against the nearest wall.

BIRD FRAME

here's a frame around picture birds
owls on branches ever dark green
barred breasts   bright talons
eyes yellow as camelias
owls in a linen nest
squared with walnut

across the room
there's a lampshade
a frame for light
gold owls are pasted on it
in a frieze of round eyes
here I take my magic hammer
with two blows start the nails
open the wood and parchment

owls blink
tree needles dangle
flurries of snow rise
to the ceiling
birds fly out the window
leaving me with the lamplight
that frames the floor in a circle

no matter how I stamp
it won't loosen
at last   at last
I drink it all up and go off
with the birds sparkling

CAMPERS

some come from another coast
some from the parched borders
of wheat towns
on Sunday they rise
into the eastern foothills
up the mountain
to the camp   to the cabin
full of stripped mattresses
like a flophouse

first the beaded slippers
then games in boxes
green shorts   new shirts soon to be
streaked with plasticene

ragged as zinnias the parents
wilt away in sedans and station wagons
Mama   Mama   the counselors are tall
strangers with strange faces
it's July when the kids
cry themselves to sleep in their bunks
nailed to the wall

NOTES FROM BONNE BAY, NEWFOUNDLAND

Table Mountain Serpentine

the wind blows
among rock ranges
over desert red flats
in gusts and lulls
under its rough surface
old men's voices
tumble and groan
like boulders torn loose

ice shines
on great bone peaks
in crevices
arctic fern drinks
and whistles
in wild trickles

down in the yellow gulch
I hear metal hairs
a power line lute
strung over old encampments
between stones I see
clumped blue bells
and the ferocious
glitter of soda cans

Winterhouse Brook Beach

the mountain's pitchers
spit nuggets of pyrite
and spout sweet water
over beach rocks

in storms when the harbor
flattens like a wet animal's back
salt water smacks up
on brook ledges

big stones
with our history crushed in
break apart
worked over
on a metamorphic shard
new lips begin to smile

graphite's black soap
opens up
ghost of bruised leaf
breathes out
from slippery pieces

when the air clears
over a clean harbor
you can see monsters
on the rock bottom

water alive and noisy
brings the mountain down

Trout River

in the steep town of Trout River
sheep graze above the church steeple
it's so poor in the town
a single power line
lights immense winters

a truck weathers overturned
on the beach among
its sea-going sisters
the dry bread of their ribs
speckled with truck rust

nails bent as old women
nap among pebbles
children with faces
like peaked roofs
shine tin blonde

back to the mountain
face to the gulf
Trout River is such a sharp place
the people wear shoes
even in summer
which is three days long

Bonne Bay Cabins

if I couldn't see the columns
of faded curtain
between huge white-framed windows
the windows wouldn't look so tall

if the white light in mornings
and sunset reflections
didn't pour through so much glass
I wouldn't see the salt bay

if it weren't so light so white so tall
with the broom
idle upright behind the oilstove
I wouldn't lie down on my closed notebook

the linking of words seems idle as the broom
when I could be
jigging for cod or throwing back
the flatfish

if it weren't so fishy grassy and light
outside so white
and warm with kettle steam inside
I wouldn't try to climb a mountain tomorrow

Table Mountain Massif

ascending a steep face
I curse each stone
I put my cheek to
and each stone rolls
under my feet

a transient crack
looks me in the eye
as another handhold crumbles
splattering my nerve
with arrowheads

just short of the peak
I quit
put my back to the mass
on the last ledge
woman   I say to myself
there's more distance
than just to the top
look at it   look away

far the good bay lies
in its poplar pocket
beyond   Gros Morne gone bald
among its spruce brothers

below   the wind yawns
an awful mouth
to fall into

Woody Point

the oilstove sings and stinks
Gros Morne across the bay
pushes through cloud
and vanishes upward
as all mountains go

under the rain's caress
sheep steam
horses bend their heads
as we did yesterday
halfway up two thousand feet
of rolling stone
and the fear of falling

we gazed down from the sun
to gulf   to town
gone today   gone   unraveled
from vision's continuous blanket
by rain and wind   memory
another mountain
forged in the spine

Tourists in Birchy Head

the reason you see no lynx or caribou
is because grief has eaten them
their pelts swing from barbed wire
rusting on human brows

precipitation is madness weeping
it falls in muddy drops
the sky is clear as truth
filled with a green ache
over the Long Range

go north to cold water to bathe
your teeth will freeze in your smile
the chattering you hear remind you
that once stones made the only noise

THREE

AMATEUR: A STORY

Love, where is love, gone to the tower
for beheading? I sit at a long bar
where a man with brown hair tells
the barkeep how he loves Brahms;
time for me to interject a clever
remark about the composer's
enormous chord clusters. Red keeps on
shining polished tumblers. The man
looks sideways at this woman who has,
he thinks, inadvertantly opened her mouth
and said something. No, he guesses again,
she said it on purpose. (Love has gone
to the tower to lose her head.)

After a quick traipse across the small
suspension bridges, Bach's Inventions,
he buys me a second drink. I sit, sip.
He tells me his name is Jim
and moves four stools over.
Only recently women have been allowed
to sit at the bar, our politicians perhaps
supposing that sin is less sweet
on her feet. (Love is stretched out in the tower,
soaking her feet in a hot tub.)

His place is further away than my place.
My place has a stove, his a hotplate.
We both play Brahms, Bach, and old
Rolling Stones to scrape off the terrible
moss that keeps gathering. Love, at this hour,
has lost her head, (also feet, naval,
and left armpit). Night strolls in formal
pleats through my groundfloor room
while he insists his name is Jim,
evidently hoping I'll call him.
Love's been thrown from the tower, foot
by breast by spine. The head sits on a spike
outside my window. She grins in.

THE WOMEN OF TOWN STREET

1

opal blue windows each one
                blanks us out
yellow plastic trellis holds up
                her sweet potato vine
dying in the sulphur kitchen dust
                no one's ever home
it seems only at midnight a naked head
                hung in the center
of the plaster sky lights up
                forty watts' worth
of territory and gold moons
                on cold beer cans

2

out   out   the cage is too small
I won't canary for you one day more
the children wear down my sill
with their hungers as they enter

out   out   into the alleys over the hills
even at a slow crawl over the weeks' shale
blisters on my knees can't hurt
more than the children's little hammers

nails   nails   hold me to the wall
all of you swing from my weight

3

old oak's been there on the corner
since an acorn among horse plops
    it's still there in a cracked circle
    behind the supermarket

summertimes the cold spit
from the market's air conditioner
    cools it and maybe at night
    it feels for the lettuces inside

4

brown house lime green door
two shutters on the left
                cracked locust shells
lodge in their hinges
dusty steps
           Annie's brownboard school floor

in pink green and yellow chalk
she writes: I love Daddy
but the steps keep turning brown

how does she know which way
they go since they go
           up and down?

5

crocks   jugs   stale biscuits
I route the gravel with a broom
               on the sills
vine leaves lie among shards
of dry paint   at dawn
sunrise shines through a green gallon
               calabrese onions hang
tattered purple
             the cat snores
nothing darkens my horizon
rain is welcome
a Blaze rose bleeds
above the door
             the reason for a rose
may be obscure but at times I know
the flower is a pause between root
and hip   the reason for roots
may be the fruit but I like to think
             the flower enough

6

the cold holds
water is dazzling in its still forms
wearing my shroud I rush from room to room
each window
a bell ringing in the sky

the winter sun
shines everywhere at once
always low and at night the Wolf Moon
blunts its fang
on the ice
as someone snarls with hunger

wearing my bridal
I crawl along corridors
carry a green moon in each finger
to see myself by

also at dawn
I lie in ditches like a piece of water
in my still form
I'm dazzling

EARLY TO FISH

Before dawn I poled my boat over
the sand bar at the river's mouth
and anchored outside. When I looked
in the water under the black string
of my handline, I saw a moon
with a long tail, a woman's face
with burning hair
riding the horizon behind her.

The coming of comets, they told me,
is so rare you'll see one, perhaps,
in a life time. What did they know,
who didn't rise early to fish,
how many comets I'd seen?
Just another face in the crowd.
I could scoop up that tailed moon.

Or catch a dozen in my dipnet,
each one thin as a layer of skin,
but their shine dies as soon
as they're lifted out.

Could have filled my bucket with comets,
and each time, a double would fall
from its side, and float.
Women are common in these waters.
Catching my living is scarce.

A POEM FOR MICHIKO

whose left hand is a bird's wing
goes with her paintbrush
in clenched right fist
to the gates of heaven for her colors
her sumi block and Chinese white
her bluegreen of broccoli
maroons of clotted blood

face to face with the faceless canvas
she paints death
and many lives
gives resuscitation's breath
to childhood's flowers and bombs

Michiko's right hand performs acrobatics
her left hand releases a bird
her heart balances at the center

CARRYING THE MORNING: A NEW ENGLAND BIOGRAPHY

Carrying the morning she walked out
of the house before her family woke,
past Mary in blue plaster set out
to grow wild by her husband's
wild French family.
                        Wet geometry sparkled
in the grass and the chickens laughed.
The rose's butter heads dropped petals
like good linen into the weeds.

It was her own hour, stolen
from yesterday's brown envelope
to pay for tomorrow; her debts
went over always to the next day.

"Grant this pleasure, that law, these dinners
on a polished table and thanks for this hour
I'd take anyway. But no," she said, "I do not
grant you, God, the tiny jar of my womb."

Across the kitchen yard stretched
her hangwoman's line, with its worn pouch
where wooden pins slept until Mondays
when she banged them shut against the sky
to hold her family up.

The family shouts would rise soon
around her, thistles taller than her head.
                        Her head was a burr
catching the light; blood, a brandy chilled
in rusty gutters, smelling of leaves.
Some nights he drank from her throat
and swore he would have another son.

Pleasure in May's first oriole song
that by June pierced her over and over
was harnessed to the men's voices,
leather reins holding the day
down to a plod.
                    Sundays,
from town the church bells bangled
respectable wrists, bright clangs, a whole
five and dime counter of trinkets
unworn when they reached her home.

Birds' song, quails' whistle, by July fell
through rotted nests, stilled. Dawns,
white hot as the damp burned.
                    She kept carrying
the mornings out long after she'd forgotten
what to do with them: peg them up
or refill the bottle or take the dead nestling
from the cat or just stand in the yard.

Light's power, August after August,
smoked her dry, strong, like a cod on a rack
down to the coast, or a wild grape pressed
for its liquor; burnt hillside, endless tending,
her best held quiet in a small bottle.
                    "Lord, God," she said,
"I'm grateful I don't strike your eye,
one marriage is enough, one day at a time
poured out, one death for a stopper."

PROVINCE OF LONELY HUNTERS: A BIOGRAPHY

When he entered the province of lonely hunters
where each man hauled on his back
the whining papoose of desires he'd planned
to leave at home,
           when he came over the hill
into their province, the air touched his nakedness.
It was enough to cool him. He said, with a spit
into the wind: "I don't need blood sports."
He took the knife from his side and threw it away.

Cold as fishes the brook ran down hill
with a couple of rocks for steps across.
He went over, and fell.
           Yellow and blue
spread on his shins, his trousers sopped,
the bugs found him. His hands came up clean,
though, even from dousing his campfire
where stones smoked like huge potatoes.

He made this trip over and over, repeating
his footsteps, as a javelin thrower
repeats his push and hurl, endlessly, all morning,
the motions laid down over each other, obliterating
earlier attempts. Bungles, falls, triumphs,
at last merged into the final execution of an act.
           He met fewer hunters
parting the leaves to look through, ferocity
driven down, banked, by age's cold cinders.

After a while he forgot the way home,
couldn't track himself back through ice water,
over burnt rock, the hill ridge, the division

of summer into its portions that led first up
a slope, then down the other side.
                        His blood simmered
a long time, drying slowly, until his kneecaps,
like old medals, lay in the grass.

THE HAIR MISTRESS

The local hair mistress burgeons
like a filled sponge,
cranks up the chair
into the mouth-to-ear streams
of refried words
that mush down just like Mexican beans.

In a coup of spray, cancer, smoke, nail polish
and farts, she's straight and combed,
the recipient of meaty dollops
ladled out over smoking basins.
Not a touch of bleach or danger
stains her impermeable smock.
Her mouth smiles a little
like a content stone,
all the same for everyone.

The women in her parlor
frilled at the stick end
like chops in a French restaurant,
wait warm and moist to be forked out
into the other world,
but even now plan to retreat again
to the soaps, shears, above all
to the whispering lover's breath
holding a womb umbrella over
their dreaming heads.

Some of us let hair grow long.
We don't want to be cut
into another shape.
The long hair indicates a sense

of self, but I know when we pass
the outside of the greenhouse
beauty glass, the hair mistress
inside averts her eyes.

They say when we're dead
our hair will grow on
so she'll get us yet.
All the same we pass,
maybe hoping something nice
will happen to our souls.

SECRETS

The wounded soldier, drab guts
spilling from his opened side,
whispers his secrets to the universe.
His cold lips continue to move
as his bowels fall folded and quiet.

The woman lying with her feet
in the stirrups describes our poor
mystery in explosions of blood
and the cannon ball of a baby's head.
She screams; nothing is private;
the doctor stitches up the torn mouth
to keep fresh news from pouring out.

In a sunken bed the old man
becomes the guest of his bones;
they hold all he is tight, tight,
as a cherishing fist; little flesh
left but the lips' purple membrane
that spills a last trickle
from his stopped spring.

The hiss of energy must be the universe
talking back over the erased tape
of soldier, mother, old man, a giving
and taking of secrets, broadcast
through the black barrel
our mote illuminates.

SOME OBSERVATIONS

1

like roads
slopes run both ways and you have a choice
of how you'll take them
    down is a frolic
    done like an otter's belly dance
on frozen snow and up
isn't always the work it seems
    up to birth or a new hat
    love's ladder or a last dream
down the long pitch to sleep
bliss at sea bottom with shells
or galaxies of electric fish
    slopes keep promising more
    than accomplished peaks

2

get up
get up the worm turns
at the surface after rain
    fish run up the river
    like rain drops or like tears
get up it's dawn in the garden
    where many mouths are busy
      among the beans
    where the lively bait is singing
    voices inaudible as air
get up this morning once again
    to watch or catch
or cry for fish pouring up the river
for their lives like you and me

3

turtles
at the end of summer days
                on the road
crushed   broken open
he who minded his own business
                in the grass
who converted greens into energy
                she who harmlessly
laid her eggs in an earth nest
unable to race but only to weigh
                as much as herself
                in her checkered box
without knocking on their neighbors
turtles exist and are bowled over

4

curls
sculpted into numbers like
                nine and two
even like three
                on the heads of holy warriors
                on their horses' necks
                        all over the plaster frieze
which time has baked to a nicotine yellow
curls thrive between bulls' horns
                on the napes of bulldancers
                ringlets   lovelocks   kisscurls
see   none on the furred bee who goes
direct to the flowery pouch

5

work
is the hand that feeds me
            in the dust of new graves
among the bent trees loaded
            with fruit
or the long slope where potatoes
boot-colored
            never stop growing
on rainy days five new words
are printed on my brow
            the ghost of my work
pressed between pages
is how you may know me

GOING FOR WOOD IN WINTER

When snow fell for two days
spirits stretched on tree branches,
slept on fence rails.
I could hear them hissing
back and forth to remind me
they'd return each winter
whether I stayed in the house
or walked out in a storm.

No fire wood left.
I went back of the hill
through great drifts;
met my father's ghost
at the oak tree, the one
with a punky wound
surrounded by beak holes.
A mess of torn woodpecker feathers
lay at the foot. That bird
must have mounted into the cloud
naked as Jesus.

Pulling the loaded sledge home
through my blue boot channels,
I thought soon enough
the saplings would take over.

All night, again, snow fell.
Between the andirons, oak embers
popped and sizzled. I lay
in the dark boughs of my life,
loving the tree.